The Power

☐ CHRISTIAN SPIRITUALITY SERIES ☐

God Under my Roof, Esther de Waal
Prayer and Contemplation, Robert Llewelyn
Learning to Pray, Mother Mary Clare SLG

*   *   *

By Brother Ramon SSF
Remember Me
Praying the Jesus Prayer
Life's Changing Seasons
Praying the Bible

*   *   *

By Tony Castle
Evelyn Underhill on Prayer
Thomas Merton on Prayer
The Prayers of Christina Rossetti
The Prayers of Lancelot Andrewes

The Power of the Name

The Jesus Prayer
in Orthodox Spirituality

Kallistos Ware
Bishop of Diokleia

My doctor is Jesus Christ,
my food is Jesus Christ,
and my fuel is Jesus Christ.

Contemporary Coptic Monk

Marshall Pickering

Marshall Morgan and Scott
Marshall Pickering
32–42 Cleveland Street
London W1P 5FB UK

First published in 1989 by Marshall Morgan and Scott Publications Ltd
Part of the Marshall Pickering Holdings Group

ISBN 0-551-01690-6

Text Set in Baskerville by Avocet Robinson, Buckingham
Printed in Great Britain by Henry Ling Ltd., at the Dorset Press, Dorchester, Dorset

Contents

Contents

1: Prayer and Silence

'When you pray,' it has been wisely said by an Orthodox writer in Finland, 'you yourself must be silent. . . . You yourself must be silent; let the prayer speak.'[1] To achieve silence: this is of all things the hardest and the most decisive in the art of prayer. Silence is not merely negative – a pause between words, a temporary cessation of speech – but, properly understood, it is highly positive: an attitude of attentive alertness, of vigilance, and above all of *listening*. The hesychast, the person who has attained *hesychia*, inner stillness or silence, is *par excellence* the one who listens. He listens to the voice of prayer in his own heart, and he understands that this voice is not his own but that of Another speaking within him.

The relationship between praying and keeping silent will become clearer if we consider four short definitions. The first is from *The Concise Oxford Dictionary*, which describes prayer as '. . . solemn request to God . . . formula used in praying'. Prayer is here envisaged as something expressed in words, and more specifically as an act of asking God to confer some benefit. We are still on the level of external rather than inner prayer. Few of us can rest satisfied with such a definition.

Our second definition, from a Russian *starets* of the last century, is far less exterior. In prayer, says Bishop Theophan the Recluse (1815–94), 'the principal thing is to stand before God with the mind in the heart, and to go on standing before Him unceasingly day and night, until the end of life.'[2] Praying, defined in this way, is no longer merely to ask for things, and can indeed exist without the employment of any words at all.

7

It is not so much a momentary activity as a continuous state. To pray is to *stand before God*, to enter into an immediate and personal relationship with him; it is to know at every level of our being, from the instinctive to the intellectual, from the sub- to the supra-conscious, that we are in God and he is in us. To affirm and deepen our personal relationships with other human beings, it is not necessary to be continually presenting requests or using words; the better we come to know and love one another, the less need there is to express our mutual attitude verbally. It is the same in our personal relationship with God.

In these first two definitions, stress is laid primarily on what is done by the human person rather than by God. But in the relationship of prayer, it is the divine partner and not the human who takes the initiative and whose action is fundamental. This is brought out in our third definition, taken from St Gregory of Sinai (+ 1346). In an elaborate passage, where he loads one epithet upon another in his effort to describe the true reality of inner prayer, he ends suddenly with unexpected simplicity: 'Why speak at length? Prayer is God, who works all things in all men.'[3] *Prayer is God* – it is not something that I initiate but something in which I share; it is not primarily something that *I* do but something that *God* is doing in me: St Paul's phrase, 'not I, but Christ in me' (Gal. 2:20). The path of inner prayer is exactly indicated in St John the Baptist's words about the Messiah: 'He must increase, but I must decrease' (John 3:30). It is in this sense that to pray is to be silent. 'You yourself must be silent; let the prayer speak' – more precisely, let God speak. True inner prayer is to stop talking and to listen to the wordless voice of God within our heart; it is to cease doing things on our own, and to enter into the action of God. At the beginning of the Byzantine Liturgy, when the preliminary preparations are completed and all is now ready for the start of the Eucharist itself, the deacon approaches the priest and says: 'It is time for the Lord to act.'[4] Such exactly is the attitude of the worshipper not only at the Eucharistic Liturgy but in all prayer, public or private.

Our fourth definition, taken once more from St Gregory of Sinai, indicates more definitely the character of this action of the Lord within us. 'Prayer', he says, 'is the manifestation of Baptism.'[5] The action of the Lord is not, of course, limited solely to the baptized; God is present and at work within all humankind, by virtue of the fact that each is created according to his divine image. But this image has been obscured and clouded over, although not totally obliterated, by our fall into sin. It is restored to its primal beauty and splendour through the sacrament of Baptism, whereby Christ and the Holy Spirit come to dwell in what the Fathers call 'the innermost and secret sanctuary of our heart'. For the overwhelming majority, however, Baptism is something received in infancy, of which they have no conscious memory. Although the baptismal Christ and the indwellng Paraclete never cease for one moment to work within us, most of us – save on rare occasions – remain virtually unaware of this inner presesnce and activity. True prayer, then, signifies the rediscovery and 'manifestation' of baptismal grace. To pray is to pass from the state where grace is present in our hearts secretly and unconsciously, to the point of full inner perception and conscious awareness when we experience and *feel* the activity of the Spirit directly and immediately. In the words of St Kallistos and St Ignatios Xanthopoulos (fourteenth century), 'The aim of the Christian life is to return to the perfect grace of the Holy and Life-giving Spirit, which was conferred upon us at the beginning in divine Baptism.'[6]

'In my beginning is my end.' The purpose of prayer can be summarized in the phrase, 'Become what you are'. Become, consciously and actively, what you already are potentially and secretly, by virtue of your creation according to the divine image and your re-creation at Baptism. Become what you are: more exactly, return into yourself; discover him who is yours already, listen to him who never ceases to speak within you; possess him who even now possesses you. Such is God's message to anyone who wants to pray: 'You would not seek me unless you had already found me.'

But how are we to start? How, after entering our room and closing the door, are we to begin to pray, not just by repeating words from books, but by offering inner prayer, the living prayer of creative stillness? How can we learn to stop talking and to start listening? Instead of simply speaking to God, how can we make our own the prayer in which God speaks to us? How shall we pass from prayer expressed in words to prayer of silence, from 'strenuous' to 'self-acting' prayer (to use Bishop Theophan's terminology), from 'my' prayer to the prayer of *Christ in me*?

One way to embark on this journey inwards is through the Invocation of the Name.

2: 'Lord Jesus . . . '

It is not, of course, the only way. No authentic relationship between persons can exist without mutual freedom and spontaneity, and this is true in particular of inner prayer. There are no fixed and unvarying rules, necessarily imposed on all who seek to pray; and equally there is no mechanical technique, whether physical or mental, which can compel God to manifest his presence. His grace is conferred always as a free gift, and cannot be gained automatically by any method or technique. The encounter between God and man in the kingdom of the heart is therefore marked by an inexhaustible variety of patterns. There are spiritual masters in the Orthodox Church who say little or nothing about the Jesus Prayer.[7] But, even if it enjoys no exclusive monopoly in the field of inner prayer, the Jesus Prayer has become for innumerable Eastern Christians over the centuries the standard path, the royal highway. And not for Eastern Christians only;[8] in the meeting between Orthodoxy and the West which has occurred over the past seventy years, probably no element in the Orthodox heritage has aroused such intense interest as the Jesus Prayer, and no single book has exercised a wider appeal than *The Way of a Pilgrim*. This enigmatic work, virtually unknown in pre-revolutionary Russia, has had a startling success in the non-Orthodox world and since the 1920s has appeared in a wide range of languages.[9] Readers of J. D. Salinger will recall the impact of the 'small pea-green cloth-bound book' on Franny.

Wherein, we ask, lies the distinctive appeal and effectiveness of the Jesus Prayer? Perhaps in four things above all: first, in its simplicity and flexibility; secondly, in its completeness; thirdly, in the power of the Name; and fourthly, in the spiritual discipline of persistent repetition. Let us take these points in order.

3: Simplicity and flexibility

The Invocation of the Name is the prayer of the utmost simplicity, accessible to every Christian, but it leads at the same time to the deepest mysteries of contemplation. Anyone proposing to say the Jesus Prayer for lengthy periods of time each day – and, still more, anyone intending to use the breathing control and other physical exercises in conjunction with the Prayer – undoubtedly stands in need of a *starets*, of an experienced spiritual guide. Such guides are extremely rare in our day. But those who have no personal contact with a *starets* may still practise the Prayer without any fear, so long as they do so only for limited periods – initially, for no more than ten or fifteen minutes at a time – and so long as they make no attempt to interfere with the body's natural rhythms.

No specialized knowledge or training is required before commencing the Jesus Prayer. To the beginner it is sufficient to say: Simply begin. 'In order to walk one must take a first step; in order to swim one must throw oneself into the water. It is the same with the Invocation of the Name. Begin to pronounce it with adoration and love. Cling to it. Repeat it. Do not think that you are invoking the Name; think only of Jesus himself. Say his Name slowly, softly and quietly.'[10]

The outward form of the prayer is easily learnt. Basically it consists of the words 'Lord Jesus Christ, Son of God, have mercy on me'. There is, however, no strict uniformity. We can say '. . . have mercy on us', instead of 'on me'. The verbal formula can be shortened: 'Lord Jesus Christ, have mercy on me', or 'Lord Jesus', or even 'Jesus' alone, although this last is less common.

13

Alternatively, the form of words may be expanded by adding 'a sinner' at the end, thus underlining the penitential aspect. We can say, recalling Peter's confession on the road to Caesarea Philippi, '. . . Son of the living God. . . .' Sometimes an invocation of the Mother of God or the saints is inserted. The one essential and unvarying element is the inclusion of the divine Name 'Jesus'. Each is free to discover through personal experience the particular form of words which answers most closely to his or her needs. The precise formula employed can of course be varied from time to time, so long as this is not done too often: for, as St Gregory of Sinai warns, 'Trees which are repeatedly transplanted do not grow roots'.[11]

There is a similar flexibility as regards the outward circumstances in which the Prayer is recited. Two ways of using the Prayer can be distinguished, the 'free' and the 'formal'. By the 'free' use is meant the recitation of the Prayer as we are engaged in our usual activities throughout the day. It may be said, once or many times, in the scattered moments which otherwise would be spiritually wasted: when occupied with some familiar and semi-automatic task, such as dressing, washing up, mending socks, or digging in the garden; when walking or driving, when waiting in a bus queue or a traffic jam; in a moment of quiet before some especially painful or difficult interview; when unable to sleep, or before we have gained full consciousness on waking. Part of the distinctive value of the Jesus Prayer lies precisely in the fact that, because of its radical simplicity, it can be prayed in conditions of distraction when more complex forms of prayer are impossible. It is especially helpful in moments of tension and grave anxiety.

This 'free' use of the Jesus Prayer enables us to bridge the gap between our explicit 'times of prayer' – whether at church services or alone in our own room – and the normal activities of daily life. 'Pray without ceasing', St Paul insists (1 Thess. 5:17): but how is this possible, since we have many other things to do as well? Bishop Theophin indicates the method in his maxim, 'The hands at work, the mind and heart with God'.[12] The Jesus Prayer, becoming by frequent repetition almost habitual and unconscious, helps us to stand in the presence of God wherever we are – not only in the sanctuary or in solitude, but in the kitchen, on the factory floor, in the office. So we become like Brother Lawrence, who 'was more united with God during his ordinary activities than in religious exercises'. 'It is a great delusion', he remarked, 'to imagine that prayer-time should be different from any other, for we are equally bound to be united to God by work at work-time as by prayer at prayer-time.'[13]

The 'free' recitation of the Jesus Prayer is complemented and strengthened by the 'formal' use. In this second case we concentrate our whole attention on the saying of the Prayer, to the exclusion of all external activity. The Invocation forms part of the specific 'prayer time' that we set aside for God each day. Normally, along with the Jesus Prayer, we shall also use in our 'set' time other forms of prayer taken from the liturgical books, together with Psalm and Scripture readings, intercession, and the like. A few may feel called to an almost exclusive concentration upon the Jesus Prayer, but this does not happen with most. Indeed, many prefer simply to employ the Prayer in the 'free' manner without using it 'formally' in their 'set' time of prayer; and there is nothing disquieting or incorrect about this. The 'free' use may certainly exist without the 'formal'.

In the 'formal' usage, as in the 'free', there are no rigid rules, but variety and flexibility. No particular posture is essential. In Orthodox practice the Prayer is most usually recited when seated, but it may also be said standing or kneeling – and even, in cases of bodily weakness and physical exhaustion, when lying down. It is normally recited in more or less complete darkness or with the eyes closed, not with open eyes before an icon illuminated by candles or a votive lamp. *Starets* Silouan of Mount Athos (1866 – 1938), when saying the Prayer, used to stow his clock away in a cupboard so as not to hear it ticking, and then pull his thick woollen monastic cap over his eyes and ears.[14]

Darkness, however, can have a soporific effect! If we become drowsy as we sit or kneel reciting the Prayer, then we should stand up for a time, make the Sign of the Cross at the end of each Prayer, and then bend from the waist in a deep bow, touching the ground with the fingers of the right hand. We may even make a prostration each time, touching the ground with our forehead. When reciting the Prayer seated, we should ensure that the chair is not too restful or luxurious; preferably it should have no arms. In Orthodox monasteries a low stool is commonly used, without a back. The Prayer may also be recited standing with arms outstretched in the form of a cross.

A prayer-rope or rosary (*komvoschoinion, tchotki*), normally with a hundred knots, is often employed in conjunction with the Prayer, not primarily in order to count the number of times it is repeated, but rather as an aid to concentration and the establishment of a regular rhythm. It is a widespread fact of experience that, if we make some use of our hands as we pray, this will help to still our body and go gather us together into the act of prayer. But quantitative measurement, whether with a prayer-rope or in other ways, is on the whole not encouraged. It is true that, in the early part of *The Way of a Pilgrim*, great emphasis is laid by the *starets* on the precise number of times that the Prayer is to be said daily: 3,000 times, increasing to 6,000, and then to 12,000. The Pilgrim is commanded to say an exact number, neither more nor less. Such attention to quantity is altogether unusual. Possibly the point here is not the sheer quantity but the inner attitude of the Pilgrim: the *starets* wishes to test his obedience and readiness to fulfil an appointed task without deviation. More typical, however, is the advice of Bishop Theophan: 'Do not trouble about the number of times you say the Prayer. Let this be your sole concern, that it should spring up in your heart with quickening power like a fountain of living water. Expel entirely from your mind all thoughts of quantity.'[15]

The Prayer is sometimes recited in groups, but more

commonly alone; the words may be said aloud or silently. In Orthodox usage, when recited aloud it is spoken rather than chanted. There should be nothing forced or laboured in the recitation. The words should not be formed with excessive emphasis or inner violence, but the Prayer should be allowed to establish its own rhythm and accentuation, so that in time it comes to 'sing' within us by virtue of its intrinsic melody. *Starets* Parfenii of Kiev likened the flowing movement of the Prayer to a gently murmuring stream.[16]

From all this it can be seen that the Invocation of the Name is a prayer for all seasons. It can be used by everyone, in every place and at every time. It is suitable for the 'beginner' as well as the more experienced; it can be offered in company with others or alone; it is equally appropriate in the desert or the city, in surroundings of recollected tranquillity or in the midst of the utmost noise and agitation. It is never out of place.

4: Completeness

Theologically, as the Russian Pilgrim rightly claims, the Jesus Prayer 'holds in itself the whole gospel truth'; it is a 'summary of the Gospels'.[17] In one brief sentence it embodies the two chief mysteries of the Christian faith, the Incarnation and the Trinity. It speaks, first, of the two natures of Christ the God-man (*Theanthropos*): of his humanity, for he is invoked by the human name, 'Jesus', which his Mother Mary gave to him after his birth in Bethlehem; of his eternal Godhead, for he is also styled 'Lord' and 'Son of God'. In the second place, the Prayer speaks by implication, although not explicitly, of the three Persons of the Trinity. While addressed to the second Person, Jesus, it points also to the Father, for Jesus is called 'Son of God'; and the Holy Spirit is equally present in the Prayer, for 'no one can say "Lord Jesus", except in the Holy Spirit' (1 Cor. 12:3). So the Jesus Prayer is both Christocentric and Trinitarian.

Devotionally, it is no less comprehensive. It embraces the two chief 'moments' of Christian worship: the 'moment' of adoration, of looking up to God's glory and reaching out to him in love; and the 'moment' of penitence, the sense of unworthiness and sin. There is a circular movement within the Prayer, a sequence of ascent and return. In the first half of the Prayer we rise up to God: 'Lord Jesus Christ, Son of God . . . '; and then in the second half we return to ourselves in compunction: ' . . . on me a sinner'. 'Those who have tasted the gift of the Spirit', it is stated in the Macarian Homilies, 'are conscious of two things at the same time: on the one hand,

18

of joy and consolation; on the other, of trembling and fear and mourning.'[18] Such is the inner dialectic of the Jesus Prayer.

These two 'moments' – the vision of divine glory and the consciousness of human sin – are united and reconciled in a third 'moment' as we pronounce the word 'mercy'. 'Mercy' denotes the bridging of the gulf between God's righteousness and the fallen creation. He who says to God, 'Have mercy', laments his own helplessness but voices at the same time a cry of hope. He speaks not only of sin but of its overcoming. He affirms that God in his glory accepts us though we are sinners, asking us in return to accept the fact that we are accepted. So the Jesus Prayer contains not only a call to repentance but an assurance of forgiveness and restoration. The heart of the Prayer – the actual name 'Jesus' – bears precisely the sense of salvation: 'Thou shalt call his name Jesus, for he shall save his people from their sins' (Matt. 1:21). While there is sorrow for sin in the Jesus Prayer, it is not a hopeless but a 'joy-creating sorrow', in the phrase of St John Climacus (+ *c.* 649).

Such are among the riches, both theological and devotional, present in the Jesus Prayer; present, moreover, not merely in the abstract but in a vivifying and dynamic form. The special value of the Jesus Prayer lies in the fact that it makes these truths come alive, so that they are apprehended not just externally and theoretically but with all the fullness of our being. To understand why the Jesus Prayer possesses such efficacy, we must turn to two further aspects: the power of the Name and the discipline of repetition.

5: The power of the Name

'The Name of the Son of God is great and boundless, and upholds the entire universe.' So it is affirmed in *The Shepherd of Hermas*,[19] nor shall we appreciate the role of the Jesus Prayer in Orthodox spirituality unless we feel some sense of the power and virtue of the divine Name. If the Jesus Prayer is more creative than other invocations, this is because it contains the Name of God.

In the Old Testament,[20] as in other ancient cultures, there is a close connection between someone's soul and his name. His personality, with its peculiarities and its energy, is in some sense present in his name. To know a person's name is to gain an insight into his nature, and thereby to acquire a relationship with him – even, perhaps, a certain control over him. That is why the mysterious messenger who wrestles with Jacob at the ford Jabbok refuses to disclose his name (Gen. 32:29). The same attitude is reflected in the reply of the angel to Manoah, 'Why askest thou thus after my name, seeing it is secret?' (Judg. 13:18). A change of name indicates a decisive change in a person's life, as when Abram becomes Abraham (Gen. 17:5), or Jacob becomes Israel (Gen. 32:28). In the same way, Saul after his conversion becomes Paul (Acts 13:9); and a monk at his profession is given a new name, usually not of his own choosing, to indicate the radical renewal which he undergoes.

In the Hebrew tradition, to do a thing *in the name* of another, or to *invoke* and *call upon his name*, are acts of weight and potency. To invoke a person's name is to make that person effectively present. 'One makes a name alive by mentioning it. The name immediately calls forth the soul it designates; therefore there is such deep significance in the very mention of a name.'[21]

Everything that is true of human names is true to an incomparably higher degree of the divine Name. The power and glory of God are present and active in his Name. The Name of God is *numen praesens*, God with us, *Emmanuel*. Attentively and deliberately to invoke God's Name is to place oneself in his presence, to open oneself to his energy, to offer oneself as an instrument and a living sacrifice in his hands. So keen was the sense of the majesty of the divine Name in later Judaism that the *tetragrammaton* was not pronounced aloud in the worship of the synagogue: the Name of the Most High was considered too devastating to be spoken.[22]

This Hebraic understanding of the Name passes from the Old Testament into the New. Devils are cast out and men are healed through the Name of Jesus, for the Name is power. Once this potency of the Name is properly appreciated, many familiar passages acquire a fuller meaning and force: the clause in the Lord's Prayer, 'Hallowed be thy Name'; Christ's promise at the Last Supper, 'Whatever you shall ask the Father in my Name, he will give it you' (John 16:23); his final command to the apostles, 'Go therefore, and teach all nations, baptizing them in the Name of the Father, and of the Son, and of the Holy Spirit' (Matt. 28:19); St Peter's proclamation that there is salvation only in 'the Name of Jesus Christ of Nazareth' (Acts 4: 10–12); the words of St Paul, 'At the Name of Jesus every knee should bow' (Phil. 2:10); the new and secret name written on the white stone which is given to us in the Age to Come (Rev. 2:17).

It is this biblical reverence for the Name that forms the basis and foundation of the Jesus Prayer. God's Name is intimately linked with his Person, and so the Invocation of the divine Name possesses a sacramental character, serving as an efficacious sign of his invisible presence and action. For the believing Christian today, as in apostolic times, the Name of Jesus is power. In the words of the two Elders of Gaza, St Barsanuphius and St John (sixth century), 'The remembrance of the Name of God utterly destroys all that is evil.'[23] 'Flog your enemies with the Name of Jesus', urges St John Climacus, 'for there is no weapon more powerful in heaven or on earth. . . . Let the remembrance of Jesus be united to your every breath, and then you will know the value of stillness.'[24]

The name is power, but a purely mechanical repetition will by itself achieve nothing. The Jesus Prayer is not a magic talisman. As in all sacramental operations, the human person is required to co-operate with God through active faith and ascetic effort. We are called to invoke the Name with recollection and inward vigilance, confining our minds within the words of the Prayer, conscious who it is that we are addressing and that responds to us in our heart. Such strenuous prayer is never easy in the initial stages, and is rightly described by the Fathers as a hidden martyrdom. St Gregory of Sinai speaks repeatedly of the 'constraint and labour' undertaken by those who follow the Way of the Name; a 'continual effort' is needed; they will be tempted to give up 'because of the insistent pain that comes from the inward invocation of the intellect'. 'Your shoulders will ache and you will often feel pain in your head', he warns, 'but persevere persistently and with ardent longing, seeking the Lord in your heart.'[25] Only through such patient faithfulness shall we discover the true power of the Name.

This faithful perseverance takes the form, above all, of attentive and frequent repetition. Christ told his disciples not to use 'vain repetitions' (Matt. 6:7); but the repetition of the Jesus Prayer, when performed with inward sincerity and concentration, is most emphatically not 'vain'. The act of repeatedly invoking the Name has a double effect: it makes our prayer more unified and at the same time more inward.

6: Unification

As soon as we make a serious attempt to pray in spirit and in truth, at once we become acutely conscious of our interior disintegration, of our lack of unity and wholeness. In spite of all our efforts to stand before God, thoughts continue to move restlessly and aimlessly through our head, like the buzzing of flies (Bishop Theophan) or the capricious leaping of monkeys from branch to branch (Ramakrishna). To contemplate means, first of all, to be present where one is – to be *here* and *now*. But usually we find ourselves unable to restrain our mind from wandering at random over time and space. We recall the past, we anticipate the future, we plan what to do next; people and places come before us in unending succession. We lack the power to gather ourselves into the one place where we should be – *here*, in the presence of God; we are unable to live fully in the only moment of time that truly exists – *now*, the immediate present. This interior disintegration is one of the tragic consequences of the Fall. The people who get things done, it has been justly observed, are the people who do one thing at a time. But to do one thing at a time is no mean achievement. While difficult enough in external work, it is harder still in the work of inner prayer.

What is to be done? How shall we learn to live in the present, in the eternal Now? How can we seize the *kairos*, the decisive moment, the moment of opportunity? It is precisely at this point that the Jesus Prayer can help. The repeated Invocation of the Name can bring us, by God's grace, from dividedness to unity, from dispersion and multiplicity to singleness. 'To stop the

23

continual jostling of your thoughts,' says Bishop Theophan, 'you must bind the mind with one thought, or the thought of One only.'[26]

The ascetic Fathers, in particular Barsanuphius and John, distinguish two ways of combatting thoughts. The first method is for the 'strong' or the 'perfect'. These can 'contradict' their thoughts, that is, confront them face to face and repel them in direct battle. But for most of us such a method is too difficult and may, indeed, lead to actual harm. Direct confrontation, the attempt to uproot and expel thoughts by an effort of will, often serves merely to give greater strength to our imagination. Violently suppressed, our fantasies tend to return with increased force. Instead of fighting our thoughts directly and trying to eliminate them by an effort of will, it is wiser to turn aside and fix our attention elsewhere. Rather than gazing downwards into our turbulent imagination and concentrating on how to oppose our thoughts, we should look upwards to the Lord Jesus and entrust ourselves into his hands by invoking his Name; and the grace that acts through his Name will overcome the thoughts which we cannot obliterate by our own strength. Our spiritual strategy should be positive and not negative: instead of trying to empty our mind of what is evil, we should fill it with the thought of what is good. 'Do not contradict the thoughts suggested by your enemies,' advises Barsanuphius and John, 'for that is exactly what they want and they will not cease from troubling you. But turn to the Lord for help against them, laying before him your own powerlessness; for he is able to expel them and to reduce them to nothing.'[27]

The Jesus Prayer, then, is a way of turning aside and looking elsewhere. Thoughts and images inevitably occur to us during prayer. We cannot stop them by a mere exertion of our will. We cannot simply turn off the internal television set. It is of little or no value to say to ourselves 'Stop thinking'; we might as well say 'Stop breathing'. 'The rational mind cannot rest idle', says St Mark the Monk,[28] for thoughts keep filling it with ceaseless chatter. But while it lies beyond our power to make this chatter suddenly disappear, what we can do is to detach ourselves from it by 'binding' our ever-active mind 'with one thought, or the thought of One only' – the Name of Jesus. We cannot altogether halt the flow of thoughts, but through the Jesus Prayer we can disengage ourselves progressively from it, allowing it to recede into the background so that we become less and less aware of it.

According to Evagrius of Pontus (+ 399), 'Prayer is a laying aside of thoughts.'[29] A *laying aside*: not a savage conflict, not a furious repression, but a gentle yet persistent act of detachment. Through the repetition of the Name, we are helped to 'lay aside', to 'let go', our trivial or pernicious imaginings, and to replace them with the thought of Jesus. But, although the imagination and the discursive reasoning are not to be violently suppressesd when saying the Jesus Prayer, they are certainly not to be actively encouraged. The Jesus Prayer is not a form of meditation upon specific incidents in the life of Christ, or upon some saying or parable in the Gospels; still less is it a way of reasoning and inwardly debating about some theological truth such as the meaning of *homoousios* or the Chalcedonian Definition. In this regard, the Jesus Prayer is to be distinguished from the methods of discursive meditation popular in the West since the Counter-Reformation (commended by Ignatius Loyola, François de Sales, Alphonsus Ligouri, and others).

As we invoke the Name, we should not deliberately shape in our minds any visual image of the Saviour. This is one of the reasons why we usually say the Prayer in darkness, rather than with our eyes open in front of an icon. 'Keep your intellect free from colours, images and forms', urges St Gregory of Sinai; beware of the imagination (*phantasia*) in prayer – otherwise you may find that you have become a *phantastes* instead of a *hesychastes*![30] 'So as not to fall into illusion (*prelest*) while practising inner prayer,' states St Nil Sorskii (+ 1508), 'do not permit yourself any concepts, images or visions.'[31] 'Hold no intermediate image between the intellect and the Lord when

25

practising the Jesus Prayer', Bishop Theophan writes. ' . . . The essential part is to dwell in God, and this walking before God means that you live with the conviction ever before your consciousness that God is in you, as he is in everything: you live in the firm assurance that he sees all that is within you, knowing you better than you know yourself. This awareness of the eye of God looking at your inner being *must not be accompanied by any visual concept, but must be confined to a simple conviction or feeling.*'[32] Only when we invoke the Name in this way – not forming pictures of the Saviour but simply *feeling* his presesnce – shall we experience the full power of the Jesus Prayer to integrate and unify.

The Jesus Prayer is thus a prayer in words, but because the words are so simple, so few and unvarying, the Prayer reaches out beyond words into the living silence of the Eternal. It is a way of achieving, with God's assistance, the kind of non-discursive, non-iconic prayer in which we do not simply make statements to or about God, in which we do not just form pictures of Christ in our imagination, but are 'oned' with him in an all-embracing, unmediated encounter. Through the Invocation of the Name we feel his nearness with our spiritual senses, much as we feel the warmth with our bodily senses on entering a heated room. We know him, not through a series of successive images and concepts, but with the unified sensibility of the heart. So the Jesus Prayer concentrates us into the *here* and *now*, making us single-centred, one-pointed, drawing us from a multiplicity of thoughts to union with the one Christ. 'Through the remembrance of Jesus Christ,' says St Philotheus of Sinai (?ninth-century), 'gather together your scattered intellect'[33] – gather it together from the plurality of discursive thinking into the simplicity of love.

Many, on hearing that the Invocation of the Name is to be non-discursive and non-iconic, a means of transcending images and thoughts, may be tempted to conclude that any such manner of praying lies altogether beyond their capacities. To such it

26

should be said: the Way of the Name is *not* reserved for a select few. It is within the reach of all. When you first embark on the Jesus Prayer, do not worry too much about expelling thoughts and mental pictures. As we have said already, let your strategy be positive, not negative. Call to mind, not what is to be excluded, but what is to be included. Do not think about your thoughts and how to shed them; think about Jesus. Concentrate your whole self, all your ardour and devotion, upon the person of the Saviour. Feel his presence. Speak to him with love. If your attention wanders, as undoubtedly it will, do not be discouraged; gently, without exasperation or inner anger, bring it back. If it wanders again and again, then again and yet again bring it back. Return to the centre – to the living and personal centre, Jesus Christ.

Look on the Invocation, not so much as prayer emptied of thoughts, but as prayer filled with the Beloved. Let it be, in the richest sense of the word, a prayer of *affection* – although not of self-induced emotional excitement. For while the Jesus Prayer is certainly far more than 'affective' prayer in the technical Western sense, it is with our loving affection that we do right to begin. Our inner attitude, as we commence the Invocation, is that of St Richard of Chichester:

> *O my merciful Redeemer, Friend and Brother,*
> *May I see thee more clearly,*
> > *love thee more dearly,*
> > *and follow thee more nearly.*

Without denying or diminishing the classic teaching of the Hesychast maters on the Jesus Prayer as a 'shedding of thoughts', it has to be acknowledged that over the centuries most Eastern Christians have used the Prayer simply as an expression of their tender, loving trust in Jesus the Divine Companion. And there is surely no harm in that.

7: Inwardness

The repeated Invocation of the Name, by making our prayer more unified, makes it at the same time more inward, more a part of ourselves – not something that we *do* at particular moments, but something that we *are* all the time; not an occasional act but a continuing state. Such praying becomes truly prayer of the *whole person*, in which the words and meaning of the prayer are fully identified with the one who prays. All this is well expressed by Paul Evdokimov (1901–1970): 'In the catacombs the image that recurs most frequently is the figure of a woman in prayer, the *Orans*. It represents the only true attitude of the human soul. It is not enough to *possess* prayer: we must *become* prayer – prayer incarnate. It is not enough to have moments of praise; our whole life, every act and every gesture, even a smile, must become a hymn of adoration, an offering, a prayer. We must offer not what we *have* but what we *are*.'[34]

The kind of prayer that Evdokimov is here describing may be defined more exactly as 'prayer of the heart'. In Orthodoxy, as in other traditions, prayer is commonly distinguished under three headings, which are to be regarded as interpenetrating levels rather than successive stages: prayer of the lips (oral prayer); prayer of the *nous*, the mind or intellect (mental prayer); prayer of the heart (or of the intellect in the heart). The invocation of the Name begins, like any other prayer, as an oral prayer, in which words are spoken by the tongue through a deliberate effort of will. At the same time, once more by a deliberate effort, we concentrate our mind upon the meaning of what the tongue says. In course of time and with the help of God our prayer grows more inward. The participation of the mind becomes more intense and spontaneous, while the sounds uttered by the tongue become less important; perhaps for a time they cease altogther and the Name is invoked silently, without any movement of the lips, by the mind alone. When this occurs, we have passed by God's grace from the first level to the second. Not that vocal invocation ceases altogether, for there will be times when even the most 'advanced' in inner prayer will wish to call upon the Lord Jesus aloud. (And who, indeed, can claim to be 'advanced'? We are all of us 'beginners' in the things of the Spirit.)

But the journey inwards is not yet complete. A person is far more than the conscious mind; besides the brain and reasoniong faculties there are the emotions and affections, the aesthetic sensitivity, together with the deep instinctive layers of the personality. All these have a function to perform in prayer, for the whole person is called to share in the total act of worship. Like a drop of ink that falls on blotting paper, the act of prayer should spread steadily outwards from the conscious and reasoning centre of the brain, until it embraces every part of ourselves.

In more technical terms, this means that we are called to advance from the second level to the third: from 'prayer of the intellect' to 'prayer of the intellect in the heart'. 'Heart' in this context is to be understood in the Semitic and biblical rather than the modern Western sense, as signifying not just the emotions and affections but the totality of the human person. The heart is the primary organ of our identity, it is our inner-most being, 'the very deepest and truest self, not attained except through sacrifice, through death'.[35] According to Boris Vysheslavtsev, it is 'the centre not only of consciousness but of the unconscious, not only of the soul but of the spirit, not only of the spirit but of the body, not only of the comprehensible but of the incomprehensible; in one word, it is the absolute centre'.[36] Interpreted in this way, the heart is far more than

29

a material organ in the body; the physical heart is an outward symbol of the boundless spiritual potentialities of the human creature, made in the image of God, called to attain his likeness.

To accomplish the journey inwards and to attain true prayer, it is required of us to enter into this 'absolute centre', that is, to descend from the intellect into the heart. More exactly, we are called to descend not from but *with* the intellect. The aim is not just 'prayer of the heart' but 'prayer of the intellect in the heart', for our varied forms of understanding, including our reason, are a gift from God and are to be used in his service, not rejected. This 'union of the intellect with the heart' signifies the reintegration of our fallen and fragmented nature, our restoration to original wholeness. Prayer of the heart is a return to Paradise, a reversal of the Fall, a recovery of the *status ante peccatum*. This means that it is an eschatological reality, a pledge and anticipation of the Age to Come – something which, in this present age, is never fully and entirely realized.

Those who, however imperfectly, have achieved some measure of 'prayer of the heart', have begun to make the transition about which we spoke earlier – the transition from 'strenuous' to 'self-acting' prayer, from the prayer which I say to the prayer which 'says itself', or, rather, which Christ sys in me. For the heart has a double significance in the spiritual life: it is both the centre of the human being and the point of meeting between the human being and God. It is both the place of self-knowledge, where we see ourselves as we truly are, and the place of self-transcendence, where we understand our nature as a temple of the Holy Trinity, where the image comes face to face with the Archetype. In the 'inner sanctuary' of our own heart we find the ground of our being and so cross the mysterious frontier between the created and the Uncreated. 'There are unfathomable depths within the heart', state the Macarian Homilies. ' . . . God is there with the angels, light and life are there, the kingdom and the apostles, the heavenly cities and the treasure of grace: all things are there.'[37]

30

Prayer of the heart, then, designates the point where 'my' action, 'my' prayer, becomes explicitly identified with the continuous action of Another in me. It is no longer prayer *to* Jesus but the prayer *of* Jesus himself. This transition from 'strenuous' to 'self-acting' prayer is strikingly indicated in *The Way of a Pilgrim*: 'Early one morning the Prayer woke me up as it were.'[38] Hitherto the Pilgrim has been 'saying the Prayer'; now he finds that the Prayer 'says itself', even when he is asleep, for it has become united to the prayer of God within him. Yet even so he does not consider that he has as yet attained prayer of the heart in its fullness.

Readers of *The Way of a Pilgrim* may gain the impression that this passage from oral prayer to prayer of the heart is easily achieved, almost in a mechanical and automatic fashion. The Pilgrim, so it seems, attains self-acting prayer in a matter of a few weeks. It needs to be emphasized that his experience, while not unique,[39] is altogether exceptional. More usually prayer of the heart comes, if at all, only after a lifetime of ascetic striving. There is a real danger that, in the early stages of the Jesus Prayer, we may too readily assume that we are passing from oral prayer to prayer of the heart. We may perhaps be tempted to imagine that we have already attained wordless prayer of silence, when in fact we are not really praying at all but have merely lapsed into vacant drowsiness of waking sleep. To guard against this, our teachers in the Hesychast tradition insist upon the need for strenuous effort when first embarking on the Jesus Prayer. They emphasize how important it is to concentrate full attention upon the recitation of the actual words, rather than to form high ambitions about prayer of the heart. Here, for eample, is the advice given by a noted spiritual father of Mount Athos, *Geron* Joseph of New Skete (died 1959):

The work of inner prayer consists in forcing yourself to say the prayer with your mouth continually, without ceasing . . . . Attend only to the words 'Lord Jesus Christ, have mercy on

31

me' . . . . Just say the Prayer aloud, without interruption . . . . All your effort must be centred on the tongue, until you start to grow accustomed to the Prayer.[44]

The significance attached here to the power of the spoken word is indeed striking. As St John Climacus tells us, 'Struggle to lift up, or rather, to enclose your thought within the *words* of your prayer.'[41] But of course we never think exclusively about the words on their own; always we are conscious also of the person of Jesus whom our words invoke.

Prayer of the heart, when and if it is granted, comes as the free gift of God, which he bestows as he wills. It is not the inevitable effect of some technique. St Isaac the Syrian (seventh century) underlines the extreme rarity of the gift when he says that 'scarcely one in ten thousand' is counted worthy of the gift of pure prayer, and he adds: 'As for the mystery that lies beyond pure prayer, there is scarcely to be found a single person in each generation who has drawn near to this knowledge of God's grace.'[42] One in ten thousand, one in a generation: while sobered by this warning, we should not be unduly discouraged. The path to the inner kingdom lies open before all, and all alike may travel some way along it. In the present age, few experience with any fullness the deeper mysteries of the heart, but very many receive in a more humble and intermittent way true glimpses of what is signified by spiritual prayer.

8: Breathing exercises

It is time to consider a controversial topic, where the teaching of the Byzantine Hesychasts is often misinterpreted – the role of the body in prayer.

The heart, it has been said, is the primary organ of our being, the point of convergence between mind and matter, the centre alike of our physical constitution and our psychic and spiritual structure. Since the heart has this twofold aspect, at once visible and invisible, prayer of the heart is prayer of body as well as soul: only if it includes the body can it be truly prayer of the whole person. A human being, in the biblical view, is a psychosomatic totality – not a soul imprisoned in a body and seeking to escape, but an integral unity of the two. The body is not just an obstacle to be overcome, a lump of matter to be ignored, but it has a positive part to play in the spiritual life and it is endowed with energies that can be harnessed for the work of prayer.

If this is true of prayer in general, it is true in a more specific way of the Jesus Prayer, since this is an invocation addressed precisely to God Incarnate, to the Word made flesh. Christ at his Incarnation took not only a human mind and will but a human body, and so he has made the *flesh* into inexhaustible source of sanctification. How can this flesh, which the God-man has made Spirit-bearing, participate in the Invocation of the Name and in the prayer of the intellect in the heart?

To assist such participation, and as an aid to concentration, the Hesychasts evolved a 'physical technique'. Every psychic activity, they realized, has repercussions on the physical and

33

bodily level; depending on our inner state we grow hot or cold, we breathe faster or more slowly, the rhythm of our heart-beats quickens or decelerates, and so on. Conversely, each alteration in our physical condition reacts adversely or positively on our psychic activity. If, then, we can learn to control and regulate certain of our physical processes, this can be used to strengthen our inner concentration in prayer. Such is the basic principle underlying the Hesychast 'method'. In detail, the physical technique has three main aspects:

(i) *External Posture.* St Gregory of Sinai advises sitting on a low stool, about nine inches high; the head and shoulders should be bowed, and the eyes fixed on the place of the heart. He recognizes that this will prove exceedingly uncomfortable after a time. Some writers recommend a yet more exacting posture, with the head held between the knees, following the example of Elijah on Mount Carmel.[13]

(ii) *Control of the breathing.* The breathing is to be made slower and at the same time co-ordinated with the rhythm of the Prayer. Often the first part, 'Lord Jesus Christ, Son of God', is said while drawing in the breath, and the second part, 'have mercy on me a sinner', while breathing out. Other methods are possible. The recitation of the Prayer may also be synchronized with the beating of the heart.

(iii) *Inward exploration.* Just as the aspirant in Yoga is taught to concentrate his thought in specific parts of his body, so the Hesychast concentrates his thought on the cardiac centre. While inhaling through his nose and propelling his breath down into his lungs, he makes his intellect 'descend' with the breath and he 'searches' inwardly for the place of the heart. Exact instructions concerning this exercise are not committed to writing for fear they should be misunderstood; the details of the process are so delicate that the personal guidance of an experienced master is *indispensable*. The beginner who, in the absence of such guidance, attempts to search for the cardiac centre, is in danger of directing his thought unawares into the area which lies below

34

the heart – into the abdomen, that is, and the entrails. The effect on his prayer is disastrous, for this lower region is the source of the carnal thoughts and sensations which pollute the mind and the heart.[44]

For obvious reasons the utmost discretion is necessary when interfering with instinctive bodily activities such as the drawing of breath or the beating of the heart. Misuse of the physical technique can damage someone's health and disturb his mental equilibrium; hence the importance of a reliable master. If no such *starets* is available, it is best for the beginner to restrict himself simply to the actual recitation of the Jesus Prayer, without troubling at all about the rhythm of his breath or his heart-beats. More often than not he will find that, without any conscious effort on his part, the words of the Invocation adapt themselves spontaneously to the movement of his breathing. If this does not in fact happen, there is no cause for alarm; let him continue quietly with the work of mental invocation.

The physical techniques are in any case no more than an accessory, an aid which has proved helpful to some but which is in no sense obligatory upon all. The Jesus Prayer can be practised in its fullness without any physical methods at all. St Gregory Palamas (1296–1359), while regarding the use of physical techniques as theologically defensible, treated such methods as something secondary and suited mainly for beginners.[45] For him, as for all the Hesychast masters, the essential thing is not the external control of the breathing but the inner and secret Invocation of the Lord Jesus.

Orthodox writers in the last 150 years have in general laid little emphasis upon the physical techniques. The counsel given by Bishop Ignatii Brianchaninov (1807–67) is typical:

We advise our beloved brethren not to try to establish this technique within them, if it does not reveal itself of its own accord. Many, wishing to learn it by experience, have damaged their lungs and gained nothing. The essence of

35

the matter consists in the union of the mind with the heart during prayer, and this is achieved by the grace of God in its own time, determined by God. The brea t hing technique is fully replaced by the unhurried enunciation of the Prayer, by a short rest or pause at the end, each time it is said, by gentle and unhurried breathing, and by the enclosure of the mind in the words of the Prayer. By means of these aids we can easily attain to a certain degree of attention.[46]

As regards the speed of recitation, Bishop Ignatii suggests:

To say the Jesus Prayer a hundred times attentively and without haste, about half an hour is needed, but some ascetics require even longer. Do not say the prayers hurriedly, one immediately after another. Make a short pause after each praycr, and so help the mind to concentrate. Saying the Prayer without pauses distracts the mind. Breathe with care, gently and slowly.[47]

Beginners in the use of the Prayer will probably prefer a somewhat faster pace than is here proposed – perhaps twenty minutes for a hundred prayers. In the Greek tradition there are teachers who recommend a far brisker rhythm; the very rapidity of the Invocation, so they maintain, helps to hold the mind attentive.

Striking parallels exist between the physical techniques recommended by the Byzantine Hesychasts and those employed in Hindu Yoga and the Sūfism.[48] How far are the similarities the result of mere coincidence, of an independent though analogous development in two separate traditions? If there is a direct relation between Hesychasm and Sūfism – and some of the parallels are so close that mere coincidence seems excluded – which side has been borrowing from the other? Here is a fascinating field for research, although the evidence is perhaps too fragmentary to permit any definite conclusion. One point, however, should not be forgotten. Besides similarities, there are also differences. All pictures have frames, and all picture-frames have certain features in common; yet the pictures within the frames may be utterly different. What matters is the picture, not the frame. In the case of the Jesus Prayer, the physical techniques are as it were the frame, while the mental invocation of Christ is the picture within the frame. The 'frame' of the Jesus Prayer certainly resembles various non-Christian 'frames', but this should not make us insensitive to the uniqueness of the picture within, so the distinctively Christian content of the Prayer. The essential point in the Jesus Prayer is not the act of repetition in itself, not now we sit or breathe, but *to whom* we speak; and in this instance the words addressed unambiguously to the Incarnate Saviour Jesus Christ, Son of God and Son of Mary.

The existence of a physical technique in connection with the Jesus Prayer should not blind us as to the Prayer's true character. The Jesus Prayer is not just a device to help us concentrate or relax. It is not simply a piece of 'Christian Yoga', a type of 'Transcendental Meditation', or a 'Christian mantra', even though some have tried to interpret it in this way. It is, on the contrary, an invocation specifically *addressed to another person* – to God made man, Jesus Christ, our personal Saviour and Redeemer. The Jesus Prayer, therefore, is far more than an isolated method or technique. It exists within a certain context, and if divorced from that context it loses its proper meaning.

The context of the Jesus Prayer is first of all one of *faith*. The Invocation of the Name presupposes that the one who says the Prayer believes in Jesus Christ as Son of God and Saviour. Behind the repetition of a form of words there must exist a living faith in the Lord Jesus – in who he is and in what he has done for me personally. Perhaps the faith in many of us is very uncertain and faltering; perhaps it coexists with doubt; perhaps we often find ouorselves compelled to cry out in company with the father of the lunatic child, 'Lord, I believe: help my unbelief' (Mark 9:24). But at least there should be some *desire* to believe;

37

at least there should be, amidst all the uncertainty, a spark of love for the Jesus whom as yet we know so imperfectly.

Secondly, the context of the Jesus Prayer is one of *community*. We do not invoke the Name as separate individuals, relying solely upon our own inner resources, but as members of the community of the Church. Writers such as St Barsanuphius, St Gregory of Sinai or Bishop Theophan took it for granted that those to whom they commended the Jesus Prayer were baptized Christians, regularly participating in the Church's sacramental life through Confession and Holy Communion. Not for one moment did they envisage the Invocation of the Name as a substitute for the sacraments, but they assumed that anyone using it would be a practising and communicant member of the Church.

Yet today, in this present epoch of restless curiosity and ecclesiastical disintegration, there are in fact many who use the Jesus Prayer without belonging to any Church, possibly without having a clear faith either in the Lord Jesus or in anything else. Are we to condemn them? Are we to forbid them the use of the Prayer? Surely not, so long as they are sincerely searching for the Fountain of Life. Jesus condemned no one except hypocrites. But, in all humility and acutely aware of our own faithlessness, we are bound to regard the situation of such people as anomalous, and to warn them of this fact.

9: The journey's end

The aim of the Jesus Prayer, as of all Christian prayer, is that our praying should become increasingly identified with the prayer offered by Jesus the High Priest within us, that our life should become one with his life, our breathing with the Divine Breath that sustains the universe. The final objective may aptly be described by the Patristic term *theosis*, 'deification' or 'divinization'. In the words of Archpriest Sergei Bulgakov, 'The Name of Jesus, present in the human heart, confers upon it the power of deification.'[49] 'The Logos became man,' says St Athanasius, 'that we might become god.'[50] He who is God by nature took our humanity, that we humans might share by grace in his divinity, becoming 'partakers of the divine nature' (2 Pet. 1:4). The Jesus Prayer, addressed to the Logos Incarnate, is a means of realizing within ourselves this mystery of *theosis*, whereby human persons attain the true likeness of God.

The Jesus Prayer, by uniting us to Christ, helps us to share in the mutual indwelling or *perichoresis* of the three Persons of the Holy Trinity. The more the Prayer becomes a part of ourselves, the more we enter into the movement of love which passes unceasingly between Father, Son, and Holy Spirit. Of this love St Isaac the Syrian has written with great beauty:

> Love is the kingdom of which our Lord spoke symbolically when he promised his disciples that they would eat in his kingdom: 'You shall eat and drink at the table of my kingdom.' What should they eat, if not love? . . . When we have reached love, we have reached God and our way is ended: we have

passed over to the island that lies beyond the world, where is the Father with the Son and the Holy Spirit: to whom be glory and dominion.[51]

In the Hesychast tradition, the mystery of *theosis* has most often taken the outward form of a vision of light. This light which the saints behold in prayer is neither a symbolical light of the intellect, nor yet a physical and created light of the senses. It is nothing less than the divine and uncreated Light of the Godhead, which shone from Christ at his Transfiguration on Mount Tabor and which will illumine the whole world at his second coming on the Last Day. Here is a characteristic passage on the Divine Light taken from St Gregory Palamas. He is describing the Apostle's vision when he was caught up into the third heaven (2 Cor. 12:2–4):

> Paul saw a light without limits below or above or to the sides; he saw no limit whatever to the light that appeared to him and shone around him, but it was like a sun infinitely brighter and vaster than the universe; and in the midst of this sun he himself stood, having become nothing but eye.[52]

Such is the vision of glory to which we may approach through the Invocation of the Name.

The Jesus Prayer causes the brightness of the Transfiguration to penetrate into every corner of our life. Constant repetition has two effects upon the anonymous author of *The Way of a Pilgrim*. First, it transforms his relationship with the material creation around him, making all things transparent, changing them into a sacrament of God's presence. He writes:

> When I prayed with my heart, everything around me seemed delightful and marvellous. The trees, the grass, the birds, the earth, the air, the light seemed to be telling me that they existed for man's sake, that they witnessed to the love of God for

man, that everything proved the love of God for man, that all things prayed to God and sang his praise. Thus it was that I came to understand what *The Philokalia* calls 'the knowledge of the speech of all creatures' . . . I felt a burning love for Jesus and for all God's creatures.[53]

In the words of Father Bulgakov, 'Shining through the heart, the light of the Name of Jesus illuminates all the universe.'[54]

In the second place, the Prayer transfigures the Pilgrim's relation not only with the material creation but with other humans:

Again I started off on my wanderings. But now I did not walk along as before, filled with care. The Invocation of the Name of Jesus gladdened my way. Everybody was kind to me, it was as though everyone loved me. . . . If anyone harms me I have only to think, 'How sweet is the Prayer of Jesus!' and the injury and the anger alike pass away and I forget it all.[55]

'Inasmuch as you have done it unto one of the least of these my brethren, you have done it unto me' (Matt. 25:40). The Jesus Prayer helps us to see Christ in each one, and each one in Christ.

The Invocation of the Name is in this way joyful rather than penitential, world-affirming rather than world-denying. To some, hearing about the Jesus Prayer for the first time, it may appear that to sit alone in the darkness with eyes closed, constantly repeating '. . . have mercy on me', is a gloomy and despondent way of praying. And they may also be tempted to regard it as self-centred and escapist, introverted, an evasion of responsibility to the human community at large. But this would be a grave misunderstanding. For those who have actually made the Way or the Name their own, it turns out to be not sombre and oppressive but a source of liberation and healing. The warmth and joyfulness of the Jesus Prayer is particularly evident in the writings of St Hesychius of Sinai (?eighth-ninth century):

41

Through persistence in the Jesus Prayer the intellect attains a state of sweetness and peace. . . .

The more the rain falls on the earth, the softer it makes it; similarly, the more we call upon Christ's Holy Name, the greater the rejoicing and exultation it brings to the earth of our heart . . . .

The sun rising over the earth creates the daylight; and the venerable and Holy Name of the Lord Jesus, shining continually in the mind, gives birth to countless thoughts radiant as the sun.[56]

Moreover, so far from turning our backs on others and repudiating God's creation when we say the Jesus Prayer, we are in fact affirming our commitment to our neighbour and our sense of the value of everyone and everything in God. 'Acquire inner peace,' said St Seraphim of Sarov (1759–1833), 'and thousands around you will find their salvation.' By standing in Christ's presence even for no more than a few moments of each day, invoking his Name, we deepen and transform all the remaining moments of the day, rendering ourselves available to others, effective and creative, in a way that we could not otherwise be. And if we also use the Prayer in a 'free' manner throughout the day, this enables us to 'set the divine seal on the world', to adopt a phrase of Dr Nadejda Gorodetzky (1901–85):

We can apply this Name to people, books, flowers, to all things we meet, see or think. The Name of Jesus may become a mystical key to the world, an instrument of the hidden offering of everything and everyone, setting the divine seal on the world. One might perhaps speak here of the priesthood of all believers. In union with our High Priest, we implore the Spirit: Make my prayer into a sacrament.[57]

'We can apply this Name to people . . . . ' Here Dr Gorodetzky suggests a possible answer to a question that is often raised: Can the Jesus Prayer be used as a form of intercession? The reply must be that, in the strict sense, it is distinct from intercessory prayer. As an expression of non-discursive, non-iconic 'waiting upon God', it does not involve the explicit recalling and mention of particular names. We simply turn to Jesus. It is true, of course, that in turning to Jesus we do not thereby turn away from our fellow humans. All those whom we love are already embraced in his heart, loved by him infinitely more than by us, and so in the end through the Jesus Prayer we find them all again in him; invoking the Name, we enter more and more fully into Christ's overflowing love for the entire world. But if we are following the traditional Hesychast pattern of the Jesus Prayer, we do not bring others before him specifically by name, or hold them deliberately in our mind, as we recite the Invocation.

All this, however, does not exclude the possibility of also giving to the Jesus Prayer an intercessory dimension. On occasion, alike in the 'free' and 'formal' use, we may feel moved to 'apply' the Name to one or more particular persons, invoking Jesus upon them as we say ' . . . have mercy on *John*'. Even if this is not exactly what the Hesychast texts envisage, it is surely a legitimate and helpful extension to the practice of the Jesus Prayer. The Way of the Name has a wideness, a generosity, not to be confined within rigid and unvarying rules.

'Prayer is action; to pray is to be highly effective.'[58] Of no prayer is this more true than of the Jesus Prayer. While it is singled out for particular mention in the office of monastic profession as a prayer for monks and nuns,[59] it is equally a prayer for laymen, for married couples, for doctors and psychiatrists, for social workers and bus conductors. The Invocation of the Name, practised aright, involves each one more deeply in his or her appointed task, making each more efficient in his actions, not cutting him off from others but linking him to them, rendering him sensitive to their fears and anxieties in a way that he never was before. The Jesus Prayer makes each into a 'man for others', a living instrument of God's peace, a dynamic centre of reconciliation.

43

Notes

1. Tito Colliander, *The Way of the Ascetics* (London 1960), p. 79
2. Cited in Igumen Chariton of Valamo, *The Art of Prayer: An Orthodox Anthology*, translated by E. Kadloubovsky and E. M. Palmer (London 1966), p. 63.
3. *Chapters*, 113 (PG 150, 1280A). See Kallistos Ware, 'The Jesus Prayer in St. Gregory of Sinai', *Eastern Churches Review* iv (1972), p. 8
4. A quotation from Psalm 118 [119]: 126. In some English versions of the Liturgy this is translated, 'It is time to do [sacrifice] unto the Lord', but the alternative rendering which we have used is richer in meaning and is preferred by many Orthodox commentators.

   The original Greek uses the word *kairos*: 'It is the *kairos* for the Lord to act'. *Kairos* bears here the special meaning of the decisive moment, the moment of opportunity: he who prays seizes the *kairos*. This is a point to which we shall return.
5. *Chapters*, 113 (PG 150, 1277D).
6. *Century*, 4 (PG 147, 637D). The idea of prayer as the discovery of God's indwelling presence can be expounded equally in terms of the Eucharist.
7. The Jesus Prayer is nowhere mentioned, for example, in the authentic writings of St Symeon the New Theologian or in the vast spiritual anthology of Evergetinos (both of the eleventh century).
8. There existed, of course, a warm devotion to the Holy Name of Jesus in the medieval West, not least in England. While this displays certain points of difference from the Byzantine tradition of the Jesus Prayer, there are also obvious parallels. See Kallistos Ware, 'The Holy Name of Jesus in East and West: the Hesychasts and Richard Rolle,' *Sobornost* 4:2 (1982), pp. 163–84.
9. It has even been translated into one of the major languages of the Indian sub-continent, Mahratti. The introduction to this translation

has been written by a Hindu university professor who is a specialist in the spirituality of the Name: see E. R. Hambye SJ, in *Eastern Churches Review* v (1973), p. 77.

10. 'A Monk of the Eastern Church' [Lev Gillet], *On the Invocation of the Name of Jesus* (The Fellowship of St Alban and St Sergius, London 1950), pp. 5–6.

11. *On stillness and the two ways of prayer*, 2 (PG 150, 1316B).

12. *The Art of Prayer*, p. 92.

13. Brother Lawrence of the Resurrection (1611–91), Barefooted Barmelite, *The Practice of the Presence of God*, ed. D. Attwater (Paraclete Books, London 1962), pp. 13, 16.

14. Archimandrite Sofrony, *The Undistorted Image: Staretz Silouan* (London 1958), pp. 40–41.

15. Quote in E. Behr-Sigel, 'Le Prière à Jésus ou le mystère de la spiritualité monastique orthodoxe', *Dieu Vivant* 8 (1947), p. 81.

16. *The Art of Prayer*, p. 110.

17. *The Way of a Pilgrim*, tr. R. M. French (London 1954), p. 29.

18. H. Berthold, *Makarios/Symeon, Reden and Briefe, Logos* B33, 2, 1: vol. ii (Berlin 1973), p. 29.

19. *Similitudes*, ix, 14.

20. See J. Pedersen, *Israel*, vol. i (London/Copenhagen 1926), pp. 245–59; but compare J. Barr, 'The Symbolism of Names in the Old Testament', *Bulletin of the John Rylands Library* 52, 1 (1969), pp. 11–29.

21. Pedersen, op. cit., p. 256.

22. For the veneration of the Name among medieval Jewish Kabbalists, see Gershom G. Scholem, *Major Trends in Jewish Mysticism* (3rd ed., London 1955), pp. 132–3; and compare the treatment of this theme in the remarkable novel of Charles Williams, *All Hallows' Eve* (London 1945).

23. *Questions and Answers*, ed. Sotirios Schoinas (Volos 1960), para. 693; tr. L. Regnault and P. Lemaire (Solesmes 1972), para. 692.

24. *Ladder*, 21 and 27 (PG 88, 945C and 1112C).

25. See Kallistos Ware, 'The Jesus Prayer in St. Gregory of Sinai' (article cited in note 3 above), pp. 14–15.

26. *The Art of Prayer*, p. 97.

27. *Questions and Answers*, ed. Schoinas, para. 91; tr. Regnault and Lemaire, para. 166.

28. *On Penitence*, 11 (PG 65, 981B). The Greek text in Migne requires emendation here.

29. *On Prayer*, 70 (PG 79, 1181C).

3o. *How the hesychast should persevere in prayer*, 7 (PG 150, 1340D).

31. *The Art of Prayer*, p. 101.

32. *The Art of Prayer*, p. 100.

33. *Texts on Watchfulness*, 27; cf. G. E. H. Palmer, Philip Sherrard and Kallistos Ware (trans.), *The Philokalia*, vol. iii (London 1984), p. 27.

34. *Sacrement de l'amour. Le mystère conjugal à la lumière de la traditon orthodoxe* (Paris 1962), p. 83.

35. Richard Kehoe OP, 'The Scriptures as Word of God', *The Eastern Churches Quarterly* viii (1947), supplementary issue on 'Tradition and Scripture', p. 78.

36. Quoted in John B. Dunlop, *Staretz Amvrosy: Model for Dostoevsky's Staretz Zossima* (Belmont, Mass., 1972), p. 22.

37. *Hom.* xv, 32 and xliii, 7 (ed. Dörries/Klostermann/Kroeger [Berlin 1964], pp. 146, 289).

38. *The Way of a Pilgrim*, p. 14.

39. *Starets* Silouan of Mount Athos had only been practising the Jesus Prayer for three weeks before it descended into his heart and became unceasing. His biographer, Archimandrite Sofrony, rightly points out that this was a 'sublime and rare gift'; not only later did Father Silouan come to appreciate how unusual it was (*The Undistorted Image*, p. 24). For further discussion of this question, see Kallistos Ware, ' "Pray without Ceasing": The Ideal of Continual Prayer in Eastern Monasticism', *Eastern Churches Review* ii (1969), pp. 259–61.

40. *Ekphrasis monastikis empeirias* (Monastery of Philotheou, Holy Mountain 1979), pp. 25–28.

41. *Ladder*, 28 (PG 88, 1132C).

42. *Mystic Reatises by Isaac of Nineveh*, translated by A. J. Wensinck (Amsterdam 1923), p. 113.

43. 'Elijah climbed to the crest of Carmel. There he crouched to the ground with his face between his knees' (1 Kings 18:42). For an illustration of a hesychast praying in this position, from a 12th century MS of John Climacus, *The Ladder of Divine Ascent*, see *The Study of Spirituality* ed. Cheslyn Jones, Geoffrey Wainwright and Edward Yarnold SJ (SPCK, London 1986), plate 3, following p. 194.

44. For further bibliography on the control of the breathing, see Kallistos

44. Ware, 'The Jesus Prayer in St. Gregory of Sinai' (cited above), p. 14, note 55. On the various physical centres and their spiritual implications, see Father Anthony Bloom (now Metropolitan of Sourozh), *Asceticism (Somatopsychic Techniques)* (The Guild of Pastoral Psychology, Guild Lecture No. 95: London 1957).

45. *Triads in defence of the Holy Hesychasts*, I, ii, 7 (ed. J. Meyendorff [Louvain 1959], vol. i, p. 97.

46. *The Arena: An Offering to Contemporary Monasticism*, translated by Archimandrite Lazarus (Madras 1970), p. 84 (translation slightly altered).

47. Op. cit., p. 81.

48. See Louis Gardet, 'Un problème de mystique comparée: la mention du nom divin (*dhikr*) dans la mystique musulmane', *Revue Thomiste*, lii (1952), pp. 642–79; liii (1953), pp. 197–216; reprinted in G. C. Anawati and L. Gardet, *Mystique musulmane: aspects et tendances – expériences et techniques* (Paris 1961), pp. 187–256.

49. *The Orthodox Church* (London 1935), p. 170 (translation altered).

50. *On the Incarnation*, 54.

51. *Mystic Treatises*, tr. Wensinck, pp. 211–12.

52. *Triads in defence of the Holy Hesychasts*, I, iii, 21 (ed. Meyendorff, vol. i, p. 157).

53. *The Way of a Pilgrim*, pp. 31–2, 41.

54. *The Orthodox Church*, p. 171.

55. *The Way of a Pilgrim*, pp. 17–18.

56. *On watchfulness and Holiness*, 7, 41, 196: cf. Palmer, Sherrard and Ware. *The Philokalia*, vol. i (London 1979), pp. 163, 169, 197.

57. 'The Prayer of Jesus', *Blackfriars* xxiii (1942), p. 76.

58. Tito Colliander, *The Way of the Ascetics*, p. 71.

59. At the clothing of a monk, in both the Greek and the Russian practice, it is the custom to give him a prayer-rope (*komvoschoinion*). In the Russian use the abbot says the following as it is handed over: 'Take, brother, the sword of the Spirit, which is the Word of God, for continual prayer to Jesus; for you must always have the Name of the Lord Jesus in mind, in heart and on your lips, ever saying: Lord Jesus Christ, Son of God, have mercy on me a sinner.' See N. F. Robinson SSJE, *Monasticism in the Orthodox Churches* (London/Milwaukee 1916), pp. 159–60. Note the usual distinction between three levels of prayer: lips, mind, heart.

Further Reading

'A Monk of the Eastern Church' [Archimandrite Lev Gillet], *The Jesus Prayer* (new edition, St Vladimir's Seminary Press, New York 1987). The best introduction to the history of the Prayer, with valuable suggestions on its practical use and detailed bibliography.

Irénée Hausherr SJ, *The Name of Jesus* (Cistercian Studies Series 44: Kalamazoo 1978). Historical; an authoritative scholarly treatment.

The Way of a Pilgrim, tr. R. M. French (London 1954). A classic nineteenth-century Russian text.

Bishop Ignatti Brianchaninov, *On the Prayer of Jesus*, tr. Fr Lazarus (London 1952). Quotes many earlier authors.

Mother Maria, *The Jesus Prayer* (Library of Orthodox Thinking, Greek Orthodox Monastery of the Assumption, Normanby 1972). Talks given by an Orthodox nun to an Anglican Benedictine Community.

Wendy Robinson, *Exploring Silence* (Fairacres Publication 36: Oxford 1974). on Prayer as listening.

Kallistos Ware, *The Orthodox Way* (Mowbrays, London and Oxford 1979). A popular general account of the doctrine, worship and life of Orthodox Christians, which raises the basic issues of Christian theology and prayer.